S0-EID-262

# *Daily* DISCIPLES

## BIBLE STUDY GUIDE

*by David Wardell, Ph.D. and Jeffrey A. Leever*
*with Ellyn Sanna*

PROMISE PRESS
An Imprint of Barbour Publishing

© 2001 by David Wardell, Jeffrey A. Leever, and Ellyn Sanna

ISBN 1-58660-062-1

All rights reserved. No part of this publication may be reproduced or transmitted in any form or by any means without written permission of the publisher.

All Scripture quotations, unless otherwise indicated, are taken from the HOLY BIBLE, NEW INTERNATIONAL VERSION®. NIV®. Copyright © 1973, 1978, 1984 by International Bible Society. Used by permission of Zondervan Publishing House. All rights reserved.

Scripture quotations marked KJV are taken from the King James Version of the Bible.

Scripture quotations marked NLT are taken from the *Holy Bible,* New Living Translation, copyright © 1996. Used by permission of Tyndale House Publishers, Inc. Wheaton, Illinois 60189, U.S.A. All rights reserved.

Scripture quotations marked NRSV are taken from the New Revised Standard Version Bible, copyright © 1989. Division of Christian Education of the National Council of churches of Christ in the United States of America. Used by permission. All rights reserved.

Scripture quotations marked THE MESSAGE are taken from *The Message.* Copyright © by Eugene H. Peterson 1993, 1994, 1995. Used by permission of NavPress Publishing Group.

Published by Promise Press, an imprint of Barbour Publishing, Inc., P.O. Box 719, Uhrichsville, Ohio 44683, www.promisepress.com

Member of the
Evangelical Christian
Publishers Association

Printed in the United States of America.

# INTRODUCTION

T his study guide is a companion to *Daily Disciples* by David Wardell and Jeff Leever. The material you are about to begin is designed to enable men and women meeting together for Sunday school or small groups to explore further the depth of material in *Daily Disciples.* Specifically, the study guide connects the content of *Daily Disciples* to Scripture. Each week's study includes a key verse, which you may want to memorize, as well as a longer passage from the Bible to read and study.

The text material in this book is original, not merely a repetition of the material in *Daily Disciples.* Although this book is meant to be a companion to *Daily Disciples,* it can also stand alone. In each chapter, you will, however, find an outline of the key points in the corresponding chapter of *Daily Disciples,* followed by that chapter's main objective, presented in the form of a weekly goal. We have also included excerpts from *Daily Disciples,* as well as quotes from other authors who speak to the same themes. For easy reference to the book, each featured quote from *Daily Disciples* gives the corresponding chapter and page number.

During each week of your study, you will have the chance to discuss or respond privately to multiple questions. All questions are directed to the individual (ideal for personal study or preparation); at the same time, they are structured for simple adaptation to group study. These questions will help apply Scripture to individual lives, so that each participant may truly become a daily disciple of Christ. Even if you are working within a group, you may find it helpful to write your answers privately, in the space allowed. You may not feel comfortable answering some of the questions in the group setting, but we encourage you to still deal with them as matters for private prayer and reflection. If you are new to study groups, you will find that trust builds as you work together longer and begin to feel more at ease with one another.

Closing applications at the end of each section are your opportunity to apply each week's material to your own personal life and situations. We encourage you to keep a written record of your responses to these applications, either in the sections labeled "Personal Reflections" or in your journal, if you keep one.

As you work through this material, remember that a study guide is just that—a *guide*. Use the material to help you grow and don't give up if you feel "stuck" on one question or issue. Keep your eyes on Jesus. He's the one we each want to follow.

May God bless your study and interaction time.

# WEEK 1

# *Getting Started*

## Read 1 Peter 1:3–9

## CHAPTER OUTLINE

I. The universal need for hope in our lives.
II. The hope that comes from being a disciple of Jesus Christ.
III. The personal implications of being Christ's disciple.

## GOAL

To understand the hope of being Christ's daily disciple.

## KEY VERSE

*Praise be to the God and Father of our Lord Jesus Christ!*
*In his great mercy he has given us new birth into a living hope. . . .*
1 PETER 1:3

> Someone once lived who made a difference. The ultimate difference.
>
> Some called him Teacher. They bore witness to the healing power of His hands. All it took was a mere touch; He could cure even the worst ailment. Yet more incredible, He could do even the impossible: He had the power to overcome death.
>
> . . .He never encountered a single soul in need of a miracle beyond what He could do for them.
>
> . . .He still brings hope to all people, all of us who at one point or another, for one reason or another, need a miracle in our lives. He is Someone Who will deliver us from the darkness.
>
> A Savior. A teacher. Someone we can learn from. *The* Teacher.
>
> He left behind a legacy. He left behind a model for *Life*.
>
> *The Answer* to our lives' confusion lies in Him.
>
> And as His body on earth—His Church—we carry this answer to each other. If we follow in His footsteps, we are His disciples. His Spirit lives in our lives, giving us the strength to *disciple* others—to reach out to others with encouragement and hope.
>
> From the prologue, *Daily Disciples*, pg. 22

All of us struggle with personal problems in our lives. No matter how great our self-confidence, we each have some private burden or trouble that we carry. We may put on a smooth, shiny façade that impresses others–but when we're all alone, when we're really honest with ourselves, we can't help but see all the areas where we fall short of being who we'd like to be. Sometimes we may get pretty discouraged.

We may have tried to change in the past. We may have tried several times. But no matter how hard we try, that same old secret (or not-so-secret) weakness trips us up. It may not be such a big thing in the eyes of others, but in our own lives it's turned into a huge thing, something far too enormous for us to simply step over and leave behind. Again and again and again, we stub our toes on the very same problem—and all too often we end up flat on our faces.

If you can relate to this description, don't give up! We're all in the same boat. Even the great heroes of the faith, the men and women we read about in the Bible, all struggled with the very same personal failures that we do. It's just human nature.

But there's good news! Jesus Christ of Nazareth offers us hope. When we become His disciples, He gives us a model to follow all the way to heaven. By His strength—not our own—we can finally leap over those obstacles that have tripped us up so many times.

> What God expects us to attempt, He also enables us to achieve.
>
> STEPHEN OLFORD

That doesn't mean that once we become Christ's disciples we will never have any more problems. Christians still struggle; they still encounter trials and difficulty. But if we keep our eyes fixed on the Person we're following, then these problems won't destroy us the way they once did. In fact, they can even make our faith in Jesus stronger. That's because step by step, Jesus will lead us forward, shielding us with His power.

Some people may think it sounds a little odd to be a disciple of a Man Who lived a couple of thousand years ago, a Person we've never even seen with our earthly eyes. But Jesus Christ is alive today. And the apostle Peter promises us that when we enter into a loving relationship with Jesus, He will fill us with inexpressible joy (1 Peter 1:8). Following Jesus is the only path that truly leads to life and happiness.

# QUESTIONS FOR STUDY AND REFLECTION

1. When you read the passage from 1 Peter, are you convinced that Jesus Christ really has the solutions to your problems? Have you ever thought of Jesus' example as something that has the answers for your daily life?

2. What is your reaction to this statement in the excerpt from *Daily Disciples:* Jesus ". . .never encountered a single soul in need of a miracle beyond what He could do for them"? Does this apply to you in any way? What miracle do you need in your own life? How does this relate to the "living hope" Peter mentions in verse 3?

3. When you look at your life in the light of Jesus Christ, do you feel hope—not only for eternity, but for your everyday life? Give examples. Do you feel that the trials you experience may actually make you stronger, as Peter describes in verses 6–7?

4. What does the phrase Peter uses, "new birth," mean to you? How does it relate to being a daily disciple of Christ?

# Closing Applications

❖ Pray during the next week that God would guide you to what He wants you to learn—that He would open your eyes to the areas that most need work. At the end of the week, record here—or in your journal if you keep one—what God has revealed to you.

❖ Make a note on your calendar or schedule to reread 1 Peter 1:3 several times this week.

❖ Make a commitment to be an active participant in this study for the next twelve weeks, writing out your thoughts and taking part in discussion. If group study is particularly challenging for you, ask another person to pray for you and hold you accountable to finishing the study now that you've started. Whom will you choose to help you be accountable?

❖ Read chapter 1 of the book *Daily Disciples* (or listen to it, if you own the audiobook version).

## Personal Reflections

_____

_____

_____

_____

_____

Consider
the model of
Jesus. He has
asked you to
follow in His
steps. . . .

DEE BRESTIN

# WEEK 2

# The Essence of Being a Daily Disciple

**Read Hebrews 5:12–6:3, Acts 2:42**

## CHAPTER OUTLINE

I. The meaning of discipleship.
II. The way to become a mature disciple:
- Through the Bible.
- Through relationships.
- Through prayer.

## GOAL

To understand that being a daily disciple is
a process of maturing in Christ.

## KEY VERSE

*Therefore let us leave the elementary teachings about Christ
and go on to maturity.*
HEBREWS 6:1

Grow up! That's really what the author of Hebrews is saying at the beginning of chapter 6. When we read the same verse in *The Message,* the meaning jumps out at us: If we're going to be Christ's disciples, then we need to stop messing around with the finger paints and start creating masterpieces.

After all, a disciple is someone who follows someone else. In our case, we want to be followers of Jesus. But we can't follow Jesus if we just sit down and refuse to go any further. Jesus wants to lead us on a journey, a lifelong adventure. Many churches place most of their emphasis on that initial decision to become Christ's disciple. But they don't talk as much about where we go from there. The Bible makes clear, though, that the Church doesn't need a bunch of spiritual babies toddling along after Jesus. No, if we're going to follow Christ, we need to be strong and mature enough to change the world. We need to step out and walk in Christ's footsteps. In the words of Hebrews, let's stop eating baby food and get down to the meat!

> So come on, let's leave the preschool fingerpainting exercises on Christ and get on with the grand work of art. Grow up in Christ. The basic foundational truths are in place.... But there's so much more. Let's get on with it!
>
> HEBREWS 6:1–3
> THE MESSAGE

To use another metaphor, imagine that the Kingdom of God is an enormous mansion filled with many rooms, each room piled high with unimaginable treasures. If we simply make a decision to follow Christ and then stop there, it's as though we went through the front door of that wonderful mansion—and then sat down on the floor and never went any further. Jesus, our loving Host, is calling us to follow Him deeper and deeper into His mansion. We don't want to miss out on all those beautiful rooms filled with bounty and grace.

So if we're going to be Christ's disciples, let's get going!

But how do we do that? That's the real question. Where do we go from here? How do we help ourselves to some spiritual meat? How do we start to explore all those rooms filled with riches?

You'll find the answer in the passage from the second chapter of Acts. Just that one verse, Acts 2:42, holds the secret. The early disciples devoted themselves to three things:

❖ *the apostles' teachings*. In our case, since we can't sit at the physical feet of the people Jesus directly taught, we need to depend on the Bible, where we can be taught from the Word of God. As we absorb Scripture into our hearts and minds, we will find ourselves changing. We will be less influenced by the world's way of thinking and we will begin thinking with God's perspectives. What's more, as we study the Bible to determine how God wants us to live our lives, we will receive wisdom and guidance as we strive to follow Jesus.

❖ *fellowship*. This means we need to develop relationships with other Christians. We're not talking here about mere social activity; we're talking about forming deep spiritual relationships that will help us to be better disciples of Jesus Christ. The disciple of Jesus is not meant to be a loner. We are each meant to be con- nected to the entire Body of Christ in practical, every- day ways as well as spiritual. God will not only use others to teach us how to be better disciples; He will also use others to express His love to us. And He'll use us the same way to bless others.

❖ *prayer.* Prayer is the way we form a living relationship with God. It doesn't have to be formal or fancy; it simply means we daily open our hearts to God.

These three things will help us follow Jesus as we explore the amazing mansion He has invited us to enjoy. Or to use the other metaphor we mentioned, these things are a big helping of spiritual meat.

## QUESTIONS FOR STUDY AND REFLECTION

1. What comes to mind when you think of the life you want for yourself as a Christian?


2. What occurs to you when you think of "spiritual milk"? What are the "fingerpainting exercises" that you've been practicing in your Christian life?


Do you. . .
❖ Find yourself typically bored with the sermon you hear on Sundays?
❖ Feel content with a Christian "life routine" that has little impact on you and others around you?
❖ Experience satisfaction simply knowing the basics about Jesus and the Bible?

3. What does the term "disciple" imply to you?
   ❖ Something academic?
   ❖ Something that sounds like work?
   ❖ Something attainable/worth pursuing?
   ❖ Something for your pastor to worry about?

4. Are you spending regular time reading and meditating on the Bible?

5. Do you have committed relationships in your life? If yes, write the names of people who come to mind. Do you think of these relationships as part of your life as a daily disciple?

6. Do you pray often? Daily?

7. How do you rank yourself in the areas of Bible study, relationships, and prayer? High? Average? Needs to improve? Would someone who knows you well rank you higher or lower in these areas? Why? What might God say about how you are doing in these areas?

# CLOSING APPLICATIONS

❖ If there is a discrepancy between the rankings you gave yourself in question 7, and how a close friend or the Lord might rank you, commit yourself to praying about this issue. Suggested prayer for the week:

*Lord, I ask You to work in my life to make me the kind of person You want me to be in all areas. I commit my will to You, and ask that You would guide me in my life as a disciple. Open my eyes to ways I can move in my life toward the kind of relationships You want for me, finding regular time in Your Word. Deepen my prayer life so that it too will become what You want for me.*

> In the Christian life, it's not how you start out that matters. It's how you finish.
>
> STEVE FARRAR

❖ Write the names of some individuals with whom you are in relationships already, but the relationships aren't the sort that are Christ-centered or disciple-oriented. As you write these names, think about each person's spiritual life. Commit yourself to praying about these relationships this week. Be open to God's leading you to begin to change these relationships in whatever way He directs.

❖ Read this week's key verse several times throughout the week. Make an effort to commit it to memory.

❖ Read or listen to chapter 2 of the book *Daily Disciples*.

# PERSONAL REFLECTIONS

If we would follow Jesus we must take certain definite steps. . . . The call to follow implies that there is only one way of believing on Jesus Christ, and that is by leaving all and going with the incarnate Son of God.

DIETRICH BONHOEFFER
*The Cost of Discipleship*

# WEEK 3

# The Cost of Daily Discipleship

Read 2 Samuel 24:18–25,
Luke 14:26–33, and Matthew 7:13–14

## CHAPTER OUTLINE

I. The cost of discipleship.
II. Getting our priorities straight.
III. The narrow gate to salvation.

## GOAL

To understand the cost of being Christ's disciple
and determine the practical ways we need to change.

## KEY VERSE

*I will not sacrifice to the LORD my God
burnt offerings that cost me nothing.*
2 SAMUEL 24:24

In the body of Christ, you can always find someone willing to tell you a version of this statement: You *should* do more (read more, evangelize more, go to church more, and so on). Is the disciple's life more of the same song? Or. . . just possibly. . .could it be. . .different?

Yes!

God has given us a wonderful opportunity to have a closer relationship with Him, an opportunity to be more like Jesus Christ. This isn't one more thing we *should* do in order to somehow prove our worth, one more thing to consume our already busy lives. Instead, this is something that enriches our lives. We benefit!

Does that mean we might have to "do something" different from what we would normally? Most likely. (That's where the cost comes in.) Yet I believe—and I think it will become clear through this book—that the disciple's life is for our own good. We're missing out on soothing medicine for our souls when we don't pursue it.

As we read in Luke, most of us have not counted the cost of this medicine. I'm not saying, however, that walking in relationship with Christ is something we can earn, something we can buy with our good behavior. No, grace is free. But to get from immaturity to maturity in the Christian life, I believe Christ must increase in our lives and we must decrease (John 3:30). We must actively pursue God's heart and will.

*Daily Disciples*, chap. 2, pg. 44

Y ou can't get something for nothing. That's the principle we hear in the passage from 2 Samuel.

God had told David to go and build Him an altar on the property of a man named Araunah. When Araunah heard why David wanted his property, he was willing to not only give him the space— he also wanted to supply the fuel and the sacrifice. But David knew that a sacrifice that had cost him nothing would not be acceptable to God. He insisted on paying for Araunah's property. Otherwise, the sacrifice would have been Araunah's rather than David's.

This may sound as though we can buy God's favor. We might

think we could even make bargains with God: *I'll do this for You, God, so You'll do that for me.* But that's not really what the Bible is saying. We can't do anything to win God's favor and love; He loves us just the way we are, with all our warts and bad habits and ugly sin. But when we choose to follow Jesus, He gives us Himself—and in return we have to surrender ourselves to Him. This is the "cost" we pay. As David knew, this is a personal transaction; no one can do it for us.

> What, then, does God watch with pleasure and delight? The man who is fighting for Him against riches, against the world, against hell, against himself.
>
> LOUIS DE MONTFORT

We need to be aware of this from the very beginning of our journey as disciples. Otherwise, we won't get very far before we'll get discouraged and turn around. In the terms Jesus used in Luke 14, we'd be like the builder who walked away with just the foundation done and no walls or roof put up.

One way to be sure we have counted the cost of being Christ's disciples is to look at our priorities. If we're following Jesus, He has to be the focus of our lives; He has to come first. If He's not, we won't really be His followers. He'll be way down the road, almost out of sight, while we're still wandering around looking at the things we think would make us happy.

Another example that might help us better understand the cost of being Christ's disciple is to think about a marriage. We don't "buy" our spouse's love—but we can't expect to get married without there being a "cost." As married people, the way we live our lives will be dramatically changed. Our focus in life will be different; our priorities will be rearranged. If that's true of a human relationship, think how much more it must apply to our relationship with Jesus Christ. We can't be His followers without a radical change in the way we live our lives.

Jesus was willing to die on the cross for us. Most of us won't be asked to die because we are His disciples—but Jesus does ask us to die to ourselves. He asks us to stop living as though we're the center of the world and instead put Him first.

In Matthew 7 Jesus uses another word picture to help us understand the cost of being His disciple. He talks about the narrow gate that leads into His Kingdom. We're not going to fit through that narrow gate if we try to carry all our selfish desires and egotistical habits with us. We're going to have to drop all that ugly baggage if we want to follow Jesus.

John Bunyan put it this way:

> I press on toward the goal to win the prize for which God has called me heavenward in Christ Jesus.
>
> PAUL, from PHILIPPIANS 3:14

*The gate is plenty wide for people who go through with nothing on their backs. But some people try to go to heaven while carrying enormous loads with them. . . . No wonder the way is much too tight.*

*Therefore, those who want to enter heaven's gate. . .must go in alone, leaving their bags of trash behind. Those who go in alone, with their hands empty, will never find the gate too small. . . .*

*The Scripture makes clear that the gate is plenty wide, so that anyone who truly wants to enter will be encouraged, knowing that God has put no unreasonable and uncomfortable restrictions along the way to heaven. But the Scripture makes just as clear that we cannot delude ourselves that we are leaving everything behind to follow God when actually we are carrying our entire lives upon our backs. We will never enter God's kingdom that way. We just won't fit.*[1]

Notice that what Christ asks us to give up turns out to be only bags of trash. We cling so tight to this stuff, you'd think we were carrying bags of gold and jewels–but when it comes down to it, it's actually all that stuff we're better off without, all the heartaches and selfishness and sin.

Jesus isn't some stingy, tight-fisted little god who doesn't want us to have any fun. No, Jesus wants us to be all that God created us to be. When we follow Him, He leads us to true joy, real peace, and absolute love. Letting go of those bulging garbage bags may seem hard–but following Jesus is well worth the cost.

## QUESTIONS FOR STUDY AND REFLECTION

1. In your own words, explain why David felt he needed to pay for Araunah's property. Can you think of any situations in your life that might relate to David's?

2. What do you think Jesus meant when He said His disciples must carry their own crosses (Luke 14:27)? In your own life, can you name one or two things that are your "cross"?

3. In Luke 14:33, Jesus says that His disciples must "give up everything." What does this phrase mean to you in practical terms?

4. As honestly as you can, list the five things that are priorities for you, in their order of importance in your life.

1. _____

2. _____

3. _____

4. _____

5. _____

Do your priorities show that you are Christ's disciple? Does the way you use your time reflect your priorities?

5. What does "counting the cost" truly mean to you? What have you given up for Jesus at this point in your daily discipleship? What baggage are you still clinging to?

6. Does your concept of the Christian life include the idea of "effort" even though grace is free? How can you follow your commitment to Christ at all costs without falling into the error of a works-oriented concept of Christianity? How would you explain this to a new Christian?

# CLOSING APPLICATIONS

❖ Pray during the coming week that God will work in your life daily, showing you in practical ways how to let go of the old baggage you've been holding onto.

❖ Record here (or in a journal, if you keep one) one specific time-consuming activity (for example, television, the Internet, computer games, hobbies, etc.) you will intentionally give up for thirty minutes at least once this week. Substitute thirty minutes of prayer or Bible reading time.

❖ Write 2 Samuel 24:24 on a note card and put it somewhere you will see it often this week—on your car's dashboard, on your computer, over your washing machine, wherever you spend a lot of time. Read it over prayerfully as often as you can. Try to commit it to memory.

❖ In the next week, make time to read or listen to chapter 3 of the book *Daily Disciples*.

## REFERENCE NOTE

[1] John Bunyan. *The Riches of Bunyan.* Updated in today's language by Ellyn Sanna (Uhrichsville, Ohio: Barbour Publishing, 1998), p. 144.

# PERSONAL REFLECTIONS

# WEEK 4

# *Relationships*

Read I Samuel 18:1–4, 20:1–4, 16–17, 41–42
*(you may want to read the entire chapters
to get the background to the story);*
Philippians 2:1–8

## CHAPTER OUTLINE

I. The effect of committed relationships on spiritual growth.
II. The dangers of isolation.
III. The need for a spirit of servanthood.

## GOAL

To understand how committed relationships–
which involve accountability and serving each other–
lead to spiritual growth.

## KEY VERSE

*Do nothing out of selfish ambition or vain conceit,
but in humility consider others better than yourselves.*
PHILIPPIANS 2:3

> When we lack a close friend, someone to whom we can be accountable, we teeter on the brink of a meltdown. Worse, when we do not have a "2 A.M." friend (one who would drop what he is doing at any time in order to meet our need), I believe we allow ourselves to miss out on God's provision for our lives. God uses other people to touch us...to bring us His love and His direction.
>
> *Daily Disciples*, chap. 3, pg. 66

Jonathan was the son of David's enemy, Saul, but Jonathan did not let this get in the way of his commitment to his friend. David feared for his life at the hands of Saul, but he knew he could trust Jonathan to help him no matter what. Their friendship was based on a mutual commitment to each other. Without that friendship, David would probably have died at Saul's hand.

*We are born helpless....We need others physically, emotionally, intellectually; we need them if we are to know anything, even ourselves.*

C. S. LEWIS

Most of us will never find ourselves in situations quite as desperate and threatening as David's—but we still need committed friends like Jonathan. Emotionally, we all need to be connected to others, or we feel lonely and isolated, but relationships like Jonathan and David's are not simply friendly, social connections. Friendships like these go far deeper. They are based on an unconditional, lifetime commitment to one another, a commitment that is founded in the Lord. When a relationship has this sort of foundation, we can dare to share both our weaknesses and our strengths; we can count on the other person to protect us and encourage us and hold us accountable for doing our very best. We can trust each other with our lives—both literally and emotionally. These are the sort of friends we need if we are to grow strong spiritually.

Satan would like to keep us isolated, separated from these strong spiritual connections. He knows that without each other, we will be weak and vulnerable to attack. As Jesus reminded us in the Gospels, "Any kingdom divided against itself will be ruined, and a house divided against itself will fall" (Luke 11:17). We cannot function as well if we are on our own—and Christ's Body, which is made up of every believer, cannot function well if the members are isolated from one another.

Think how silly it would be if the various parts of a human body tried to act independently from the rest. The foot would go hopping off on its own, the eye would sit all alone, and the stomach would insist on digesting food by itself. The image is ludicrous, of course, and absolutely impossible; the various body parts couldn't exist at all, let alone function, if they didn't have each other. The same is true of us. We need each other.

In a similar way, David needed Jonathan if he hoped to survive Saul's insane plots to kill him. Saul would have liked to drive a wedge between Jonathan and David; Saul knew David would be more vulnerable without Jonathan's protection. But Jonathan would not back out of his commitment to his friend. We need to have "Jonathan friends"—and we need to be that kind of friend to others.

> A friend is always loyal ...born to help in time of need.
>
> PROVERBS 17:17
> NLT

Most of us already have plenty of relationships in our lives—but those relationships may not measure up to Jonathan and David's standard. How can we take our friendships deeper? How can we turn them into the kind of committed relationships that will help us grow spiritually?

If we look at Jonathan's commitment to David, we see that it involved action, not just words. The Scripture says over and over that Jonathan loved David as he loved himself. This meant that Jonathan looked out for his friend the same way he looked out for himself. He went out of his way to be of service to David.

This attitude of willing service is what sends our relationships into a deeper, more spiritual level. When we stop putting our own selfish interests first, we will find our friends are no longer merely casual acquaintances.

Jonathan's commitment to David is the same sort of relationship that Paul describes in the second chapter of his letter to the Philippians: humble. . .selfless. . .like Christ Jesus. Jesus was so absolutely committed to us that He became our servant. And then He humbled himself still further and gave up His very life.

When we begin to follow Christ's example, we'll find our relationships grow deeper pretty quickly. And then–together–we can impact the world.

Typically, we don't see an instant transition where I move from self-focus to focusing on others. This sort of change does not come quickly or easily. It requires self-discipline. It require a whole new mind-set. . . . We aren't particularly naturally predisposed to being good candidates for this. But the burden was never meant to be carried alone. When we labor together, even the hardest work becomes a little easier.

*Daily Disciples*, chap. 3, pg. 63

# QUESTIONS FOR STUDY AND REFLECTION

1.  What do you think was the foundation for David and Jonathan's relationship (common interests, goals, work, church)? How did they take their friendship deeper?

2.  Do you have a "Jonathan" in your life already? What relationships in your life would you like to deepen?

3.  In what ways do you feel isolated? What circumstances have caused you to feel separated from others? What practical steps can you take to bring unity to your relationships?

4.  What is your attitude toward serving others? Is this something you want to do—or is it hard for you to contemplate? Why?

5.  When you think about the people in your life, who has acted as a servant toward you in practical ways? Describe what they have done.

6.  What are some practical ways you can serve your friends (including your spouse, if you have one)? If you begin to do these things, do you think your relationships will change? How? Will you grow closer to the Lord as well? Why or why not?

## CLOSING APPLICATIONS

❖ List the names of friends and relatives (either here or in a journal, if you keep one) with whom you would like to have a more committed relationship. Pray each day this week for these individuals and ask God to deepen your commitment to them.

❖ Write Philippians 2:3 on a note card and put it somewhere you will see it often this week. Read it prayerfully as many times as you can. Try to commit it to memory.

❖ Go back to your list of people to whom you want to be more committed. After each name, write one practical action you can take this week to serve that person. Check off each action as you accomplish it and record any results or thoughts that strike you.

❖ In the next week, make time to read or listen to chapter 4 of the book *Daily Disciples*.

# PERSONAL REFLECTIONS

As iron
sharpens iron,
a friend sharpens
a friend.

PROVERBS 27:17 NLT

# WEEK 5

# *Mentoring and Discipleship*

## Read Ecclesiastes 4:9–12

## CHAPTER OUTLINE

I. Definition of three kinds of
committed spiritual relationships:
• Mentor.
• Encouragement/accountability partner.
• Protégé.
II. Seeking out a mentor.
III. Maintaining proper balance and accountability
within the mentoring relationship.

## GOAL

To understand and experience
committed spiritual relationships.

## KEY VERSE

*Though one may be overpowered,*
*two can defend themselves.*
*A cord of three strands is not quickly broken.*
ECCLESIASTES 4:12

> I'm convinced every person needs someone who knows them well and offers them regular encouragement—but also loves them enough to challenge them and ask tough questions when they are warranted. This obviously doesn't mean, though, that when we start up a new friendship, we levy all sorts of criticism against the other person based on our own personal convictions. But when a solid relationship built on trust has been established, then this part of the disciple's life can take place.
>
> *Daily Disciples,* chap. 4, pg. 74

We get more work done when we work together.

This is a simple fact of life we all know is true when it comes to the concrete jobs of daily life. If you have a helper, you can accomplish more, go further, climb higher. When you get tired, the other person can take over; when the other person tires, you step in. The fact that you're not alone encourages you when you feel like giving up, adds excitement when you're going strong, and keeps you from feeling lonely when the work is hard and long.

The same principles apply to our spiritual journey. We are not meant to "go it alone." The Christian life is built around relationships. If we want to follow Jesus, then we need to accept help from His other followers–and in return, we need to help those who are struggling along beside us.

Ecclesiastes 4:12 speaks of a cord made up of three strands. If

> I make it a practice to surround myself with trusted people who have walked further down the heavenly road. . . . I also make it a practice to take under my wing those who are needing to climb some of the same mountains I've already traversed.
>
> LAURIE HALL

you've ever worked with rope or yarn, you know that three strands wrapped tightly around each other are far stronger than a single strand. The same is true in our own lives as disciples. We can think of the three strands as three different types of spiritual relationships:

❖ *mentor,* an older person (or one who is more mature in Christ) who encourages and instructs us

❖ *encouragement/accountability partner,* a fellow disciple who is an equal with us

❖ *protégé,* a younger person (or one who is less mature in Christ) whom we encourage and instruct

Ideally, we all would be involved in at least one of each of these types of committed spiritual relationships.

What if you look around you, though, and there just doesn't seem to be anyone who could offer one of these types of relationships? Then make it a priority to seek out people who want to commit themselves to walking together as Christ's daily disciples. You're not too likely to bump into people like this at your local bar; you may not be able to find them at work; but you should run into them at church, particularly in a small-group Bible study or fellowship group. Ask God to help you. He wants you to have these relationships in your life, so you can count on Him to bring them into being.

But even though we need each other—and we really do—we also need to remember that as disciples we are not following any human being, nor do we want anyone else to follow us. We are all called to follow Jesus, and we need to keep our eyes on Him. So when we accept the guidance of a mentor, we are still responsible for checking in first and foremost with Christ for His direction. And when we mentor someone else, we need to encourage our protégés to do the same. It may be comforting to look to a human being for all our encouragement and leadership—and it may also be a real stroke to our egos to have someone less experienced look to us that way. But God's will as revealed in the Scripture needs to be our final standard.

> We should not attempt to "get this Christian life right" out on our own. Even knowing that we will always face risks in any human (therefore never infallible) relationship, we simply cannot afford to become isolated. Isolation is the result of either outright relationship avoidance or resistance to God's voice telling us to pursue something deeper for already-existing relationships. The outcome of either is typically worse than the risks we face in relationships.
>
> *Daily Disciples*, chap. 4, pg. 81

## QUESTIONS FOR STUDY AND REFLECTION

1. Is there someone in your life who mentors you? Who? Give examples of ways this person provides you with leadership and insight.

2. Do you have an encouragement/accountability partner? Who? How does this person encourage you? How does he or she hold you accountable?

3. Are you and your encouragement/accountability partner comfortable not only praising each other for a good job but also confronting each other with gentleness? How could you become more comfortable, more open with each other?

4. Do you have someone you teach and encourage? If so, how do you mentor this person? If not, can you think of anyone you know who might appreciate your mentoring? How can you deepen this relationship further?

5. One of the risks of leading others is that we sometimes tend to be judgmental. What are some practical ways that we can avoid this danger?

6. What other hazards are involved with a mentoring relationship? How can we avoid them?

# CLOSING APPLICATIONS

❖ List the names of your mentors, accountability/encour-
agement partners, and protégés (either here or in your
journal, if you keep one). Throughout this week pray
specifically for each relationship. Thank God for the way
these individuals have enriched your life.

❖ Write Ecclesiastes 4:12 on a note card and place it where
you will see it often. Reread it throughout the week. Try
to memorize it if you can.

❖ Next to each name you wrote in response to the first
application, write one practical action you will take this
week to encourage or express your appreciation for that
person (for instance, write a note, make a phone call,
send an E-mail, visit, etc.) Follow through and record the
responses to your actions.

❖ Read or listen to chapter 5 of *Daily Disciples*.

# PERSONAL REFLECTIONS

_____

_____

_____

_____

_____

_____

The Christian life should not—cannot—be lived in lonely isolation. Faith is no do-it-yourself project.

TIMOTHY JONES

# Week 6

# *The Word*
# *(and Your Vision)*

Read John 17:20–23;
1 Corinthians 10:31–11:1; James 1:5–6

## Chapter Outline

I. Seeing the way God sees.
II. Helping each other see.
III. Developing a personal vision statement.

## Goal

To understand God's vision and learn how to
develop and follow a personal vision statement.

## Key Verse

*Where there is no vision, the people perish. . . .*
Proverbs 29:18 kjv

> How are we going to stay on that narrow path that Christ mentioned in the book of Matthew? I don't think we can if we lack a sense of spiritual direction. Our life as Christians is a journey toward Christlikeness. Having a personal vision is what starts us and sustains us along the road.
>
> *Daily Disciples,* chap. 5, pg. 87

When it comes to being Christ's disciple, it doesn't really matter how well our eyes function. What really matters is this: Can we "see" Jesus well enough to follow Him?

All sorts of things can get in the way of our seeing Jesus: emotional things like fear and selfish desires, concrete things like bills and responsibilities and material possessions. But when we stop seeing as the world sees and begin seeing as God sees, we'll find our spiritual vision becomes clearer

> Is there anything worse than blindness? Oh, yes! A person with sight and no vision.
>
> HELEN KELLER

and clearer as we go along. If we want to be Christ's daily disciples, then we need to have His vision for our lives.

The verses in John 17 show us the vision Jesus had for each of us. This is the prayer He brought to His Father on the night before His death, and the words show us how much He loves us. He wants each of us to be united with all His other followers, just as He and His Father are one. This unity is Jesus' vision for us all.

Accomplishing Christ's vision all by ourselves is very difficult. We may say that we want to do everything for God alone, and forget about the rest of the world—and of course this desire has some value. But ultimately as we serve God, we have to work together, just as the verses in 1 Corinthians tell us. If we do every-thing for God's glory, then we will set an example that others can follow. Working together, we should help each other to "see" more clearly.

Of course all of us should have one single focus for our lives: to glorify God and follow Christ. But we each live that out in different ways, as God calls us. He has given us unique gifts, unique long-ings, unique ways we serve Him best. Defining our own personal vision statements will help us be more clear about what those unique gifts and longings are. It will help us be more focused on what God wants for our lives. It will make us more effective disci-ples of Christ.

Sometimes your vision statement may be as simple as the answer to the question, "What is it that you want to do?" What is it you hope to achieve, both in your personal walk with God and in the Church? Other times, you may want to write out a more detailed plan for your life that summa-rizes your vision. Either way, by putting your vision into words, you make it more concrete. If you put your vision statement somewhere you will see it often, you will remind yourself of the direction you want your life to take. As Howard Hendricks has said, "Aim at nothing, and you will hit it every time." We don't want our lives to be aimless and haphaz-ard; we want to shoot true and straight at the target God wants for us.

> The vision is not a castle in the air, but a vision of what God wants you to be.
>
> OSWALD CHAMBERS

Since your vision statement is so important, it cannot be devel-oped quickly or automatically. Instead, spend time in prayer asking God what He wants for your life. The verses in James 1 promise us that God will give us wisdom when we ask Him for it. He will show us the direction He wants our lives to take.

The best way to be sure that you are choosing the direction God wants for your life is to spend time searching the Scriptures. Your vision statement needs to be firmly based on God's Word, the Bible. Trust God to help you truly "see." He will make clear to you His vision for your life.

## QUESTIONS FOR STUDY AND REFLECTION

1. Using the passage from John 17, describe in your own words Jesus' vision for each of us. Does His vision change the way you see the Christian life? In what way?

2. What are some practical ways others have helped you "see" Jesus more clearly? What are some practical things you can do to help others "see"?

3. If you do not already have a personal vision statement, what are the concrete steps you need to take to develop one (see the Closing Applications section for some ideas)? If you do have a vision statement, how do you find it affects your daily life?

4. As you think about your personal vision, what part does the Bible play? In what ways do you find that the Bible gives you direction?

## Closing Applications

❖ Set aside some time this week to pray specifically about your personal vision statement. If you already have one, ask God to give you the strength to live out your vision consistently in your daily life. If you don't have your own vision statement yet, ask God to reveal to you what His vision is for your personal life.

❖ Write Proverbs 29:18 on a note card and put it somewhere you will see it often throughout the week. Read it over prayerfully many times. Try to memorize it.

❖ Either here or in a journal (if you keep one) make a list of your goals for your life. Then make another list of the things you love to do the most, the things you do with all your heart. Is there a "common thread" that runs through these two lists? How do they fit in with God's vision for your life? Use that common thread to write a simple one-sentence personal vision statement. Copy that statement on a note card and put it somewhere you will see it often.

❖ Read or listen to chapter 6 of *Daily Disciples*.

# PERSONAL REFLECTIONS

_____

_____

_____

_____

_____

_____

_____

_____

_____

_____

_____

_____

_____

_____

_____

_____

_____

_____

_____

_____

_____

_____

_____

And whatever you do, whether in word or deed, do it all in the name of the Lord Jesus, giving thanks to God the Father through him.

COLOSSIANS 3:17

# WEEK 7

# *Prayer*

## Read Luke 2:21–28, 36–38; 11:1–13

## CHAPTER OUTLINE

I. The necessity of prayer.
II. Praying continually.
III. Praying as Jesus did.

## GOAL

To understand prayer and learn to pray as Jesus did.

## KEY VERSE

*Ask and it will be given to you;*
*seek and you will find;*
*knock and the door will be opened to you.*
MATTHEW 7:7

Prayer isn't a hidden talent. All it takes is a willingness to spend the time to do it. In the daily disciple's life, prayer is a core element that holds the other pieces together.

*Daily Disciples*, chap. 6, pg. 101

Have you ever prayed for something day after day, month after month, year after year—and still not received an answer from God? If so, many times you probably felt frustrated and discouraged. You were probably tempted to give up. Common sense would tell you that was the most sensible thing to do.

But the two individuals in this week's Scripture reading didn't listen to common sense. Both Simeon and Anna had heard the Holy Spirit prompting them—and both of them had been obedient in prayer, year after year. Their prayers were focused on God, rather than on themselves, so they could simply rest in God's presence, worshiping Him as they relied on His strength to bring the answer to their prayers.

> None can believe how powerful prayer is, and what it is able to effect, but those who have learned it by experience.
>
> MARTIN LUTHER

Luke tells us that Anna never left the temple; night and day, she was there worshiping God and praying. God will probably not ask you and me to spend our entire lives in our local church building, wearing out our own little spot on the carpet beside our favorite pew—but we can still be like Anna. Anna was an old woman who had lived a long and painful life—and yet she chose to remain constantly in God's presence, praising Him. And we, too, can make that same choice. Day and night, no matter where we are, we can open our hearts to God, bringing to Him both our petitions and our praise. We don't need to be physically in a church building; we don't need to close our eyes or get down on our knees; we don't even need to say specific words or any words at all. We may pray in all of these ways sometimes—but we don't *have* to do any of those things to be like Anna. Instead, we simply have to make a conscious effort to turn our attention to God, to silently offer up to Him the desires of our hearts, and to give Him gratitude and praise. And when we do, eventually, in God's time (not ours), He will show us the answer to our prayers. Like Anna and Simeon, we will see Christ revealed in our lives.

There's no way we can truly follow Jesus without spending time in prayer. The Gospels make clear that even the Son of God needed to renew His relationship with God again and again by slipping away by Himself to spend time alone in prayer with His Father. His disciples had seen Him in prayer so often that in Luke 11 they asked Him to share with them the way they ought to pray. That was when He taught them what we have come to know as the Lord's Prayer.

If you read over the lines of this prayer, you will see that it includes both praise and practical concerns. We are to make God's name holy; we are to pray that God's kingdom will come to earth—and in the next breath Jesus lets us know that we can also talk to God about our "daily bread"—all those ordinary, everyday needs and worries.

Be joyful always; pray continually; give thanks in all circumstances, for this is God's will for you in Christ Jesus.

I THESSALONIANS 5:16–18

In Luke 11 we hear Jesus compare prayer to the human relationships between friends or between parents and children. As friends, we listen when our friends talk to us; as parents, we love to give our children the good things they need. If we selfish human beings answer each other with love, how much more attentively will our heavenly Father listen to us when we speak to Him? How much more lovingly will He bestow His blessings on us when we ask Him?

Prayer may not come easily or naturally to us, however. No matter how good our intentions, we are all so easily distracted by the noise and busyness of our lives. We need to discipline ourselves to spend regular time in God's presence, but even then we may feel "stuck," as though nothing much is happening during those quiet times alone. Or we may feel we had a wonderful time of prayer—only to feel our closeness to God slip away as soon as we go back to our lives' responsibilities and concerns. It's safe to say that most of Jesus' disciples have had these experiences at one time or another. When we run into these problems, though, the passage in Luke 11 can give us hope and encouragement. We can ask God for *anything*, Jesus promised us, and He will hear and answer. We can even ask for His help in our prayer life.

So if you feel as though your prayer life is not going anywhere, if you find yourself unable to live in a constant state of prayer as Anna did, simply offer even that up to Jesus. Ask Him for His help. Seek the answer to your dilemma. Keep on knocking on heaven's door.

> When you pray, go away by yourself, shut the door behind you, and pray to your Father secretly. Then your Father, who knows all secrets, will reward you.
>
> MATTHEW 6:6 NLT

Jesus promised that when we ask with our whole hearts we will be answered; when we seek with our whole being we will find what we have been looking for; and when we knock and knock and knock and never give up knocking, He will fling open the door and invite us into His presence.

And remember—Jesus always keeps His promises.

Just as God honored the prayers of His Son and the prayers of Anna, so He will honor the prayers of men and women who daily live as His disciples. God gave us the privilege to communicate with Him; we have the honor of praying to Him for our own needs and also on behalf of others. Of course, we cannot coerce, manipulate, or force God to answer our desires. We *can* ask Him anything, and then allow Him to answer our prayers in His own timing and will. The prayer of a righteous man or woman is effective, especially when we take the time to align our prayers with God's purposes.

*Daily Disciples,* chap. 6, pg. 105

## QUESTIONS FOR STUDY AND REFLECTION

1. Why should we pray?

2. Have you ever prayed for something for a long time without receiving an obvious answer? How did you feel? When Anna and Simeon at last received the answer to their prayers, what does the Gospel say they each did?

3. When you examine your own prayer life honestly, does most of your communication with God consist of petitions for something you want? Do you also, like Anna and Simeon, remember to praise God for His answers?

4. According to 1 Thessalonians 5:17, we are to pray continually. What does continual prayer mean to you? Have you ever experienced it? If so, how is continual prayer lived out in your daily life? Do you think continual prayer is an attitude or an activity?

5. 1 Samuel 12:23 reminds us that an important part of our daily relationship with God includes prayer for others. How important do you think it is to pray for others? When you think about an individual, do you pray for him or her?

6. Billy Graham has stated, "If you do not feel like praying, it is probably a good indication that you should start praying immediately." Has there ever been a time in your life when you didn't feel like praying, but you opened up to God anyway? What was the result?

## CLOSING APPLICATIONS

❖ Do you want to learn to pray? Do you want an attitude of prayer? Begin by asking God to help you. You might want to make this your prayer for the week:

*Lord, I ask You to teach me to pray—not as an activity nor as a way to earn Your love. Please, simply teach me to have an attitude of prayer. Remind me to pray for others. May my heart be filled with Your praise.*

❖ Write the names of some individuals who come to mind, people who may be a part of your daily life, people you love, even people with whom you may be feeling angry or upset. Ask God to show you the needs in these people's lives. Commit yourself to praying for these individuals when they come to mind this week.

❖ Write this week's key verse on a note card and place it where you will see it often as you go about your life. Reread it as many times as you can. Try to memorize it.

❖ Read or listen to chapter 7 of the book *Daily Disciples*.

## PERSONAL REFLECTIONS

_____

_____

_____

_____

_____

_____

_____

_____

_____

WEEK 8

# Opportunities for Action

### Read Luke 24:13–33

## CHAPTER OUTLINE

I. The disciple's life as an ongoing process.
II. The value of God-given opportunities to grow through our
encounters with specific events and people.
III. Making a conscious choice to move forward
in our walk as disciples.
IV. Making ourselves available as opportunities arise,
so that God can use us for growth in the lives of others.

## GOAL

To embrace the idea that God puts people and events
before us as opportunities for us to grow,
so that we, too, can be available to others.

## KEY VERSE

*Therefore, prepare your minds for action. . . .*
1 PETER 1:13

The disciple's life is a *process*. Along the way, though, are small events that by themselves may not seem that significant. But in the scope of the Kingdom they can work together to create a masterpiece, a "finished" product—the mature believer.

*Daily Disciples*, chap. 7, pg. 117

Choosing to be Christ's disciple is not one of those landmark events you do once and then never have to do again. Instead, it's an ongoing thing. That's why we talk about *daily* disciples—because we have to make a choice to follow Jesus each and every day. It's a day-by-day, lifelong process, a process that transforms us into Christ's image as we make the choice step by step to follow Him.

Like the disciples in this week's Scripture, we, too, are walking a road, making a journey from our old location to a brand-new place. Choosing this road, however, is not like stepping onto a conveyor belt that will just automatically carry us to our destination. Instead, all along the way, God gives us opportunities for action, places where we have a choice to make. The choices we make at these points will shape the direction of our entire lives.

There is never a coincidence in the life of a Christian.

HENRY BLACKABY

These opportunities don't come into our lives with a bolt of lightning from heaven. Usually, they come to us quietly, disguised in the shapes of the people we meet and the events that take place in our lives. Sometimes we may barely realize the chance God is giving us to grow. But at each of these life events, we have a choice: We can choose not to take advantage of this opportunity for growth—or we can choose to follow Jesus.

A host of opportunities for action can be gleaned from the story of the Road to Emmaus. Consider the following:

❖ *Get into relationships with a few others.* The two disciples on the road to Emmaus were spending time together, even in their confusion and sadness.

❖ *Communicate through prayer and Scripture on spiritual and heart issues.* These two disciples spent time with Jesus discussing the Scriptures, and together with Jesus they came to God in prayer before their meal.

❖ *Allow Jesus to direct your walk; seek and search after the Father's will.* These disciples asked Jesus to accompany them on their journey, and they were clearly open to the insight He gave them.

❖ *When you spend time with other disciples, keep things focused on Christ.* Jesus asked, "What are you discussing together as you walk along?" Their response tells us that they had been talking about Jesus and the event that led to His death.

❖ *Put your trust in God.* These disciples were dismayed by the Crucifixion, but Jesus reminded them to see things from God's perspective rather than a human one.

❖ *Enter into Christ's suffering and brokenness.* These two disciples could think of nothing besides Jesus' death.

❖ *Let Christ open your eyes to His plans—His opportunities for action—for you.* Because these two individuals had been open to what Jesus had to say to them, their eyes were opened and they saw the truth.

❖ *Express to God your willingness to be sent, and embrace His call.* These two people immediately went back to Jerusalem to tell the others the good news. Read Isaiah 6:8–9.

❖ *Open the Scriptures to others.* Luke 24:32 says, "They asked each other, 'Were not our hearts burning within us while he talked with us on the road and opened the Scriptures to us?' "

❖ *Ask Christ to stay with you and be your guide.* We don't know the rest of the story, but after their experience with Jesus on the road to Emmaus, it's likely that these two disciples walked with Him daily.

❖ *Understand the message Christ left the disciples; find opportunities to share it.* If we read on past this story a few verses, Luke 24:47 says, "And repentance and forgiveness of sins will be preached in his name to all nations, beginning at Jerusalem."

❖ *Stay together and struggle together.* Again, we don't know the specific details of these two individuals' lives, but we do know that all the disciples spent time gathering together, sharing their hardships and triumphs.

The disciples on the road to Emmaus had an opportunity to grow. Why? Because Christ made Himself available to them. When He did, they made the choice to make themselves available to others as well, to spread the Good News to the other disciples.

We, too, as the Lord's disciples, have a choice to make: Will we take advantage of our opportunities for action? Will we not only grow in our own lives, but will we make ourselves available to others, so that they, too, can choose to grow because of us?

## QUESTIONS FOR STUDY AND REFLECTION

1. What was the mind-set of the disciples on the road to Emmaus? What was their focus? What is your mind-set in your relationships? What is your focus?

2. In the passage from Luke, did the disciples' focus change once Jesus revealed Himself? How? Does your focus change as you encounter Christ or as He reveals something to you? How?

3. Based on what you know about the young church, were these disciples' lives enriched by the choices they made? Were others' lives enriched? How?

4. Think of the opportunities for growth in your own life story. As they unfold, how might these opportunities enrich your life and the lives of others?

5. List one or two opportunities for action that God has put into your life in the past. How did you respond? What action did you take?

6. Are you aware of any current opportunities for growth in your life right now? If so, what are they? What action will you take?

Bit by bit, little by little, as we invest more, we will experience a deepening of spiritual maturity. One small step may be all we need to get us moving in the right direction today. Whenever we move in the direction God wants, at each point—each step—we can find an expanded vision of His purposes, an increase in our own confidence, and a heightened zeal and joy in our lives.

*Daily Disciples*, chap. 7, pg. 121

## CLOSING APPLICATIONS

❖ Are you willing to recognize the opportunities God puts before you? Do you want to respond with action? If so, begin by focusing on God. You might want to pray this prayer (or something similar) every day this week:

*Lord, thank You for giving me the desire to enrich my relationships with You and others. Help me to be aware of opportunities You give me. Help me to obey and respond with action.*

❖ This week intentionally make yourself available to others. Write the name below of an individual or event in your daily life that you recognize as an opportunity for action on your part. Record the specific action you chose to take (or plan to take) and then record the events as they unfold.

❖ Write this week's key verse on a note card and place it somewhere you will see it often. Read it through as many times as you can this week. Try to memorize it.

❖ Read or listen to chapter 8 of the book *Daily Disciples*.

## PERSONAL REFLECTIONS

_____

_____

_____

_____

_____

_____

_____

_____

_____

_____

_____

_____

We must be re-
fashioned as a liv-
ing whole in the
image of God. . . .

DIETRICH BONHOEFFER

# Reconciliation

## Read 2 Corinthians 5:17–21 and 1 Corinthians 12:14–26

## CHAPTER OUTLINE

I. The meaning of reconciliation:
God no longer counts our sins against us.
II. Christ's disciples as His ambassadors,
called to spread His message of reconciliation,
overcoming divisions or differences.
III. Working together as "one body."

## GOAL

To recognize subtle as well as blatant divisions
within the body of believers and become unified,
effective ambassadors for Christ.

## KEY VERSE

*All this is from God,*
*who reconciled us to himself through Christ*
*and gave us the ministry of reconciliation. . . .*
2 CORINTHIANS 5:18

> Reconciliation has everything to do with being a disciple. In a spiritual sense, reconciliation means that God has not counted our sins against us, but has forgiven us through Christ. In an interpersonal sense, reconciliation means if we have anything against our brother or sister, we are to "leave the altar" (Matthew 5:23–24) and go be reconciled to our brother or sister.
>
> *Daily Disciples*, chap. 8, pg. 127

As Paul says in the passage from 2 Corinthians 5, we are new creations in Christ. The old creation was separated from God by human sin and selfishness—but the new creation is no longer far from God. Through Christ, God moved our ugly sin out of the way, so that we could come close to Him. He made us into new people, people who have been radically transformed and healed. This is the message of the gospel, the Good News of Christ.

> If you are offering your gift at the altar and there remember that your brother has something against you... First go and be reconciled to your brother; then come and offer your gift.
>
> MATTHEW 5:23–24

But the gospel doesn't stop there. The Good News isn't meant just for you and me—it's meant for everybody. God wants us to spread His message of reconciliation to the world. He wants us to be His ambassadors. He wants to send His love out to the world through our hands and feet and mouths.

This means that we can no longer let differences come between us and other people. We can't be God's ambassadors and judge our fellow human beings on the basis of their race or gender or education or job—or anything at all. Christ's ministry of reconciliation breaks down all the walls that have so long divided us from one another.

If you hug to yourself any resentment against anybody else, you destroy the bridge by which God would come to you.

PETER MARSHALL

Unfortunately, some of the most obvious walls are right inside the church itself. We look down on those who believe differently than we do; we think we have nothing in common with people who worship God in ways that seem strange to us. Sometimes the divisions lie along denominational lines, but other times we put up walls within our own local church communities. We point our fingers and talk behind people's backs. We get our feelings hurt and allow resentment to separate us from our fellow believers. We let our differences become more important than our common goal as Christ's disciples.

Clearly, this isn't what God wants. Instead, as Paul explains in 1 Corinthians 12, God wants His people to act as though they were *one body*. This means that we are all interconnected; we all depend on each other. Even the smallest and humblest are just as essential to the body's health as the most prominent and talented.

We can spread Christ's message of reconciliation far more effectively when we, as His disciples, are united into one living and loving body.

---

Through *reconciliation*, we *become* representatives or ambassadors of Christ, so God can reach others with the gospel through us. If we are not first reconciled to our heavenly Father, we cannot live the disciple's life.

How, then, do we develop or attain a reconciling spirit? We don't. But as we yield ourselves to the Lord Jesus Christ, He can make a positive difference in others through us. It's not about our efforts; it's about God working through our lives.

*Daily Disciples*, chap. 8, pg. 127

# QUESTIONS FOR STUDY AND REFLECTION

1. In your own words, describe what you feel Paul meant when he speaks of God's ministry of reconciliation.

2. What are some concrete ways that we can be Christ's ambassadors to the world? What are some small, everyday ways that we can represent Christ to those around us?

3. Obviously, the Corinthian believers were experiencing division among their members. Do we have division in our churches today? What types of problems do we find among believers?

4. Are you aware of any division that is holding you or your church back from growing in Christ? Do you see an attitude of jealousy or pride toward other believers? What issues can we work at as we interact with people different from ourselves?

5. Is there anyone with whom you need to reconcile? What practical steps should you take to reach reconciliation?

6. Why is our unity so important to the watching world?


## Closing Applications

❖ Do you embrace God's call to a ministry of reconciliation? Do you see any areas of division in your life? Use this—or a similar prayer in your own words—each day this week:

*Lord, please help me to be aware of the divisions in Your body. Forgive me for any unloving attitudes I have toward others. Grant me the courage to reconcile with all of Your followers so that together we will be effective witnesses to Your world.*

❖ This week be sensitive to the Holy Spirit's nudging you to reconcile with other believers. On the page that follows (or in your journal, if you keep one), write the name of an individual with whom you have had a misunderstanding or from whom you feel estranged, even in a small way. Write the steps you will take to reconcile with that individual. Record your thoughts and the individual's response to your actions.

❖ Write this week's key verse on a note card and place it somewhere you will see it often. Read it over prayerfully as many times as you can this week. Try to memorize it.

❖ Read or listen to chapter 9 of *Daily Disciples*.

# PERSONAL REFLECTIONS

_____

_____

_____

_____

_____

_____

_____

_____

The Lord calls us
to be instruments
of reconciliation
as well as to be
reconciled where
there may be a
division, an
estrangement, a
misunderstanding.

HENRY GARIEPY

_____

_____

_____

_____

_____

# Passing on the Mantle

Read 2 Timothy 2:1–7, 10, 14–16, 22–26

## CHAPTER OUTLINE

I. Giving "the blessing" to our children.
II. Finding time for our children.
III. Using the Word as our guide as we pass a
spiritual legacy to the next generation.

## GOAL

To accept the responsibility of passing on
a spiritual legacy to the future generation.

## KEY VERSE

*We will tell the next generation
the praiseworthy deeds of the LORD,
his power, and the wonders he has done.*
PSALM 78:4

From the very beginning, Yahweh has made clear how much He wants us to "pass on the mantle." But we can't force this mantle onto our children. The goal should always be that the next generation absorbs Scripture, rather than has it force-fed to them.... Children need to see what Scripture means in their parents' lives....

*Daily Disciples,* chap. 9, pg. 149

Imagine what the world would be like today if the apostle Paul had not passed on his spiritual legacy to the next generation. If faith in Christ had died with that first Christian generation, you and I would never have had the chance to know Jesus for ourselves. Christianity would have faded away before it could transform the world.

Timothy was not Paul's flesh-and-blood son, but Paul couldn't have loved him more if he were. Paul discipled the younger man; he encouraged him and prayed for him and taught him all he knew about the Lord. In a real way, he gave his "blessing" to this young man.

As parents—or simply as mentors who are older and wiser—we, too, can give a blessing to those who are younger. We may do this informally, in many ways, every day—but oftentimes a special formal blessing can make our spiritual legacy more real and concrete, both to the young person in question and to ourselves. This blessing puts into words all that we pray and hope for the next generation—and it has real spiritual meaning and power.

> These commandments that I give you today are to be upon your hearts. Impress them on your children.
>
> DEUTERONOMY 6:6–7

In this week's Scripture reading from 2 Timothy 2, Paul gives Timothy some practical advice. This letter is one way Paul passed his mantle on to Timothy—but we can learn from his words as well. As we read these verses, we find some excellent pointers for handing on our own spiritual legacy.

As we interact with the younger generation, here are some of Paul's key points to keep in mind:

❖ First of all, remember that Jesus Christ is our only source of strength. We can rely on His power, both in our own lives and in the lives of our children. He will never let us down.

❖ Read Scripture often. Know what the Bible says—and then pass it along to the next generation.

❖ Be willing to endure hardship. Interacting with the younger generation isn't always easy. It takes time and effort; there are no shortcuts. But our goal—our children's salvation—is worth it all.

❖ Make sure your life is a constant reminder of God's grace. The younger generation should be able to see God's power at work in your life. You should be willing to talk openly about your faith—but remember, your actions are far more powerful than your words. Be one of God's honest workmen; young people are quick to spot a hypocrite.

> Train a child in the way he should go, and when he is old he will not turn from it.
>
> PROVERBS 22:6

❖ When you do talk, be careful what you say. It's easy to

let our tongues run away from us. Choose your words prayerfully, especially when the younger generation is listening.

❖ Teach the younger generation how to avoid the temptations that go along with being young. Share with them the wisdom of your own experience. Don't be afraid to be honest about the times you made foolish choices; young people can learn from our mistakes.

❖ Set an example of living peacefully with others; don't allow yourself to be caught up in quarrels. Teach the young people you know how to avoid senseless arguments. Most of all, avoid power struggles and arguments with the younger generation.

❖ Instruct the younger generation gently. Remember that God alone can lead them to knowledge of the truth. Trust them to Him.

Whether we have biological children of our own or not, we, too, like Paul, can pass on our spiritual mantle to the next generation.

## QUESTIONS FOR STUDY AND REFLECTION

1. What can we learn from Paul and his example of passing on the mantle? What steps should we take in our lives to invest in the younger generation? Should we rearrange our priorities?

2. Have you ever formally "blessed" your children (or another young person in your life)? What did this blessing include? What were the effects of it (both practically and spiritually)? If you have never had this experience, do you think it is something you would like to try? Why or why not?

3. Are you spending time with members of the younger generation? How? As young people watch you, can they see Scripture and its principles at work in your life?

4. When you were a child, did you have someone who "passed the mantle" to you? What were the circumstances? What effect did that individual have on your life?

5. How are you investing in the future generation? Whether or not you are a parent, what opportunities do you have to pass on a spiritual legacy?

# Closing Applications

❖ Do you accept the responsibility of passing your spiritual legacy to the future generation? This week, daily offer up this prayer to the Lord (or pray something similar in your own words):

*Lord, thank You that children are a heritage from You. I humbly accept the responsibility to pass on my mantle of faith. Help me to invest in the lives of children and give my blessing so future generations will trust You.*

❖ Throughout this week, prioritize your investments. Commit to spending time with children so they will absorb Scripture's principles through your life. Write the names of your children and/or at least one other child who has a chance to observe your daily life. Record the tangible ways you will bless each young person and pass on your legacy.

❖ Write the key verse on a note card and place it where you will see it often this week. Read it several times and try to commit it to memory.

❖ Read or listen to chapter 10 of the book *Daily Disciples*.

You may not think you have any opportunity to pass on your heritage of faith to the younger generation—but look around you. There may be a young person with whom you have contact who needs your love and influence.

*Daily Disciples,* chap. 9, pg. 152

# PERSONAL REFLECTIONS

WEEK 11

# Multiplication and Small Groups

**Read Acts 2:42–47**

## CHAPTER OUTLINE

I. The role of "lifestyle discipleship" in the early church.
II. Informal relationships as a means to spread the gospel.
III. Small groups as a powerful technique
for multiplying believers.

## GOAL

To understand the impact small informal groups
can have on multiplying the number of Christ's disciples.

## KEY VERSE

*And let us consider how we may spur one another
on toward love and good deeds.
Let us not give up meeting together,
as some are in the habit of doing,
but let us encourage one another—
and all the more as you see the Day approaching.*
HEBREWS 10:24–25

> The gospel of Christ is one of love—and how can we demonstrate our love if we are not in close, committed relationships with others? Small groups are one opportunity we have to form and build a network of love and commitment between the members of Christ's body.
>
> That's why small groups are also such a powerful way to spread the Good News of Jesus.
>
> *Daily Disciples*, chap. 10, pg. 157

As we see in this week's Scripture reading, the early church understood how important it was for them to get together. When you read these verses, you get the impression that the fellowship and the meals were just as important as the miracles and the doctrine. The close relationships within this small group were part of what made it so powerful. People around them could see they weren't like everybody else; they could see they truly loved each other. This intimacy and honest love made other people want to join them. Because of the early church's "lifestyle discipleship," more and more people came to Jesus each and every day.

> May God grant us joy as we strive earnestly to follow the way of discipleship. May we be enabled to say "No" to sin and "Yes" to the sinner.
>
> DIETRICH BONHOEFFER

Things aren't so different today. When we interact with people informally, they have a chance to get to know who we really are. Hopefully, they will see Jesus at work in our lives. Better yet, they will feel His love reaching out to them through us.

Here are some practical ways to spread the gospel through informal relationships:

- ❖ *Faithfulness.* Be reliable, someone who can be counted on at all times.

- ❖ *The ability to listen.* Make sure others "have your ear" when they need it. Take things in rather than speak frequently.

- ❖ *Integrity.* Be straightforward. Don't allow impure motives to taint your actions.

- ❖ *Naturalness.* Demonstrate transparency and sincerity.

- ❖ *Understanding.* Be willing to give the benefit of the doubt. Look for ways to understand rather than criticize.

- ❖ *Eternity-focused.* Relate to others, remembering always that souls matter more than anything.

- ❖ *Trustworthiness of speech.* Make sure your yes means yes, and your no means no. When you say you are going to do something, the listener can take your word to the bank. Keep your promises.

- ❖ *Encouragement.* Communicate positively rather than focusing on the negative; be on the lookout for ways to express appreciation toward others. "Major" in praising people.

If we belong to a large church, it may be difficult to form the warm, close relationships that were typical of the early church. Our formal church services may be wonderful worship experiences—

but they may not always be conducive to casual friendships and intimate caring. But small groups can encourage the informal friendships that can spread Christ's Good News so powerfully.

These small groups should:

❖ share and apply the truth from God's Word;

❖ pray and intercede for one another; and

❖ use experiences from the group to develop maturity in Christ.

Small groups that put these three things in practice become power vehicles for multiplying Christ's disciples.

## QUESTIONS FOR STUDY AND REFLECTION

1. In what ways is your church similar to the early church as it is described in Acts 2? In what ways is it different?

2. What were the results of the early church's fellowship? How were the believers affected? How did it affect those outside of the fellowship? What do you think would happen if we were to follow the early church's example more closely?

3.  In what ways do you use your informal relationships to spread the Good News? For example, do you, like those in the early church, invite others to your home for fellowship? What other action do you take?

4.  How do you interact with others? Do you listen and encourage and understand? Do you have integrity in your relationships? How do you demonstrate love? Are you only concerned with "spiritual" needs, or do you give to those in physical need?

5.  Should we persevere in small group relationships? Why? What may result? If you have been in a small group before, list some practical ways you personally have grown because of your involvement.

6.  What are some challenges that small groups face? Have you experienced any difficulties in the context of small groups? How might we overcome these problems?

# CLOSING APPLICATIONS

❖ Do you agree with the concept of multiplying the Church? Are you devoted to the apostles' teaching, fellowship, breaking of bread, and prayer? If you want this sort of fellowship to play an important part in your life as Christ's disciple, offer God this prayer (or a similar one in your own words) each day this week:

*Lord, I thank You for allowing me to be part of Your Church. I want to be devoted to You. Please use my relationships to multiply Your Church.*

❖ Make time this week to meet with other believers for teaching, fellowship, breaking of bread, and prayer. Ask God to use these activities to increase His Church. Write down an individual's name and the specific action you will take to demonstrate Christ's love to this person. (You may want to consider inviting him or her to join a small group fellowship. Or you may want to strengthen in some other way the informal relationship you have with this person.)

❖ Write the key verse on a note card and place it somewhere you will read it often this week. Try to memorize it.

❖ Read or listen to chapter 11 of the book *Daily Disciples*.

# PERSONAL REFLECTIONS

Dear friends,
since God so
loved us, we also
ought to love
one another.

1 JOHN 4:11

Love is taking the
initiative and act-
ing sacrificially to
meet the needs
of others.

DARYL DALE

# WEEK 12

# *Leadership*

## Read 1 Timothy 3:1–12; Philippians 2:3–8

## CHAPTER OUTLINE

I. The need for spiritual leaders.
II. Servanthood as an essential element of
Christian leadership.
III. The importance of keeping human leadership
in its proper perspective.

## GOAL

To understand the need for
servant-oriented leadership within the body of Christ.

## KEY VERSE

*Your attitude should be the same as that of Christ Jesus.*
PHILIPPIANS 2:5

Along our path as daily disciples, we are called to have godly influence on others' lives. Leadership is a part of this, for influence and leadership are intertwined.

*Daily Disciples*, chap. 11, pg. 173

Leadership is an important part of being Christ's disciple. We are not all called to be pastors or deacons or other formal leaders—but Christ wants each of us to be ready and willing to lead those around us. If we lack self-confidence—and most of us do to some extent—the word "leadership" may sound scary. But it's really just a question of sharing our wisdom. . .of influencing those around us for good.

> We need people in our lives to challenge us, to inspire us to greater depths of passion and greater heights of commitment.
>
> BILL MCCARTNEY

In this week's Scripture reading from 1 Timothy, Paul is telling his young protégé the necessary requirements for Christian leadership. Surprisingly enough, Paul doesn't say anything about spiritual leaders needing to have a dynamic personality—nor does he say they have to be good speakers or be self-confident extroverts. He *does* say that spiritual leaders should be experienced Christians who are deeply committed to their spouses and children. That intimate, personal integrity is what makes someone a good candidate for Christian leadership.

That's not usually how the world chooses its leaders, but as Christ's disciples we are following His example rather than the world's. As we read in the verses from Philippians 2, Christ's version of leadership is very different from anything the world offers.

His leadership is humble and selfless. The greatest leader the world ever had came to us as a servant, eager and willing to give Himself away. In the same way, we, too, can be strong leaders to those around us when we are willing to be of service to them.

Many of the world's most well-known leaders have also been some of the most arrogant people. For these individuals, leadership proved to be the ultimate ego trip. But Jesus was willing to make Himself nothing for our sakes—and as His disciples we, too, are called to do the same.

*Leading* is very different from *pushing*. Sometimes we confuse the two, but servant-oriented leadership always respects the other person's right to decide. If we're following Christ's example, we won't cram our values down anyone's throat, even when we think we know better than the other person what is right for his or her life.

> Help us, O God, to do our best to help other people to accomplish and to achieve, knowing that their contribution is what God is trying to give the world.
>
> FLORENCE SIMMS

In the Corinthian church, at the time of Paul's first letter to them, believers were confused about the concept of leadership. Some argued, "I'm a disciple of Paul." Others said, "I am a disciple of Apollos." Still others claimed, "Peter is the one I follow." A few of them got it right: *"I follow Christ."*

No matter who is leading and who is following within the Church, we are all disciples of Jesus. The younger or less experienced people I may lead are not *my* disciples. Nor am I a disciple of those who help me know the way I should go. Instead, each of us is following Christ. We are *His* disciples. Keeping Christ as our ultimate leader gives us a healthy perspective on spiritual leadership. As the verses after this week's Scripture remind us, "at the name of Jesus every knee should bow. . .and every tongue confess that Jesus Christ is Lord" (Philippians

2:10–11). He alone can lead us to eternal life.

> We can all be a leader to somebody, whether our spouses, children, siblings, friends, coworkers—chances are, someone is looking up to us. Biblically, we have the responsibility and calling to be good leaders. We can either accept it or ignore it.
>
> *Daily Disciples,* chap. 11, pg. 183

## QUESTIONS FOR STUDY AND REFLECTION

1. Why does Christ's body need leaders? What happens when we lack leaders?

2. Why do you think Paul stressed to Timothy the importance of strong family commitments? How do you think this quality relates to leadership?

3. What personality traits automatically come to mind when you think of leadership? Are these the same traits that Paul describes in Philippians 2? Why do you think the world's concept of leadership is so different from Christ's?

4. Have you known any human leaders who followed the model described in Philippians 2? If so, describe these individuals. What were the effects of their leadership?

5. Even if our normal circumstances don't suggest we'd be the most likely leaders, we can lead others in the right direction. List people (leaders) who influenced you. Also, is there someone you're influencing?

6. Why are spiritual leaders so scarce? Are we too busy waiting for someone else to take over? Are we simply too busy? Are we concentrating on our own weaknesses rather than God's strength?

## CLOSING APPLICATIONS

❖ What are your thoughts today regarding the issue of leadership in the body of Christ? Have you ever viewed yourself as a leader? Do you think others might view you that way? Each day this week offer God this prayer (or a similar one in your words):

*Lord Jesus, thank You for modeling leadership to the Church. Thank You for being willing to empty Yourself and become a servant. Show me who You want me to influence. . .and remind me to always have a servant's attitude as I develop in leadership.*

❖ This week, think of the leaders in your life who have influenced you—leaders both in official capacities and in relationships. Write their names and the influence they have made on you. Also ask God to show you who you are leading or influencing, and write their names. Pray specifically for each person this week and look for ways to be a servant in these people's lives. Record the results of your actions here or in your journal (if you keep one).

❖ Write the key verse on a note card and place it some-where you will see it often this week. Read it prayerfully as many times as you can. Try to memorize it.

❖ Read or listen to chapter 12 of *Daily Disciples*.

> There are multitudes of unsung heroes—people who the world never noticed as leaders, but who made all of the difference for Christ in other people's lives. They are truly "the greatest leaders," because they were humble and focused on Jesus; they cared about others and acted out their love in concrete ways.
>
> *Daily Disciples*, chap. 11, pg. 184

# PERSONAL REFLECTIONS

_____

_____

_____

_____

_____

_____

_____

Man looks at the
outward appear-
ance, but the
LORD looks at
the heart.

I SAMUEL 16:7

_____

_____

_____

_____

_____

_____

_____

_____

_____

# Not a 100-Meter Dash but a Marathon

### Read Hebrews 12:1–13

## CHAPTER OUTLINE

I. The disciple's life as a journey.
II. Finding the strength to persevere.
III. Our lives as memorials of God's work.

## GOAL

To view life as a journey, not a short burst,
so that our lives will be a living testimony
to God's loving power.

## KEY VERSE

*Let us throw off everything that hinders and
the sin that so easily entangles,
and let us run with perseverance
the race marked out for us.*
HEBREWS 12:1

> We don't become discipled Christians through any single encounter—anymore than athletes can prepare for the Iron Man Triathlon in one training session.
>
> *Daily Disciples,* chap. 12, pg. 190

Discipleship is a journey. The author of the Book of Hebrews describes it like a race.

If you've ever tried running with weights on your ankles, you know how much harder it is to pick up speed when you have five pounds dragging at each foot. Sin and selfishness in our lives have the same effect on the spiritual race we're running: They're like heavy weights hanging around our ankles, slowing us down.

We all have our share of sin. But this week's Scripture calls us to allow Christ to cut the weights off our ankles so we can follow Him with quick, light feet. Typically, it's a lifelong process. We have to persevere even when giving up seems so much easier. We have to keep running no matter how many times we stumble.

But we don't run alone. That's the good news. Jesus Christ is our companion. He gives us strength when we tire and encouragement when we feel like giving up. He was the One Who first planted the seed of faith in our hearts–and when we keep our eyes fixed on Him, He will bring our faith to maturity.

Our brothers and sisters in Christ are with us in this race as well. From them we can also draw power and encouragement. Together, we strengthen the "feeble arms and weak knees," and we make "level paths" for our feet (Hebrews 12:12–13). Day by day, together, we run the marathon of faith.

Just as athletes train for a big race, we, too, can gather strength for our spiritual marathon. Our "training" happens during the time we spend in prayer and reading the Word (focusing our eyes on Jesus)—and it also happens during the time we spend in fellowship with other believers. These activities will help us run the race before us with greater endurance.

> Instant Christianity tends to make the faith act terminal and so smothers the desire for spiritual advance.... No single encounter between God and a creature made in His image could ever be sufficient to establish an intimate friendship between them.
>
> A. W. TOZER

Sometimes we all get discouraged, but one way to stay active in the disciple's daily marathon is to keep our end goal always in mind. If you knew your life would end today, what would you want (or what could you expect) your family or friends to engrave on your headstone? Think about it. Is your life a testimony to Christ's grace, a permanent memorial of His love and power? Or is it a testimony to something else?

*Are you following Christ daily?*


# QUESTIONS FOR STUDY AND REFLECTION

1. In what ways is the disciple's life like a race?

2. What are some elements of the disciple's "training" for the marathon of faith?

3. In your own life, what are some "weights" that tend to trip you up?

4. What are some practical ways you can keep your eyes fixed on Jesus?

5. In your words, explain how Jesus is the "author and perfecter of our faith."

6. In what way is your life a "memorial" to Christ's grace? Could you be a better testimony for Jesus? What would need to change?

## CLOSING APPLICATIONS

❖ Do you view your walk with Christ as a marathon? Do you persevere? Do you want to influence others in your life so that your life will be a memorial of Christ's grace? This week, offer God this prayer (or pray something similar in your own words):

*Lord, thank You for the privilege of traveling through life with You beside me—thank You that I don't have to run this race alone. Give me the strength to persevere and the courage to act in faith. May my life be a living testimony to Your love and grace.*

❖ Write your epitaph as you hope you will be remembered after you die. What do you want your legacy to be?

❖ Write this week's key verse on a note card and put it somewhere you will read it often throughout the week. Try to memorize it.

❖ Over the past weeks, what are the most important things you have learned from this Bible study? Write them here (or in your journal, if you keep one). Has this study changed the way you live your life in any practical ways? If so, how? How will you continue to apply the principles of being a daily disciple?

---

We are called to a daily life of disciplehood, not just an awakening.

The disciple's life starts one person at a time, one family at a time, one church at a time, one community at a time. . .and then one nation at a time. The legacy Christ left with His disciples is an ongoing one—to the glory of God.

What a legacy He has left us! By any measuring standard, Jesus' legacy stands alone. . . . Christ began with twelve men. Today millions know His name.

*Daily Disciples,* chap. 12, pg. 191

# PERSONAL REFLECTIONS

_____

_____

_____

_____

_____

_____

_____

Oh, that my steps
might be steady,
keeping to the
course you set.

PSALM 119:5
THE MESSAGE

_____

_____

_____

_____

_____

_____

_____

_____

_____

# ABOUT THE AUTHORS

**David Wardell** is the cofounder of the international ministry Promise Keepers and currently serves as ambassador-at-large. Dave earned his Ph.D. at the University of Utah. He has also served as an assistant professor at the University of Colorado and has taught at Kansas State University.

**Jeff Leever** has worked as a writer and editor for numerous publications. He currently serves as editor for *Men of Integrity,* a devotional magazine copublished by Promise Keepers and *Christianity Today.* Formerly senior editor for Promise Keepers, Jeff now acts as manager of publications.

**Ellyn Sanna** is the author of more than forty books. She speaks at women's retreats and mothers' groups and works as a full-time freelance editor. She and her family make their home in upstate New York.

# ALSO AVAILABLE FROM
# DR. DAVID WARDELL AND JEFFREY A. LEEVER

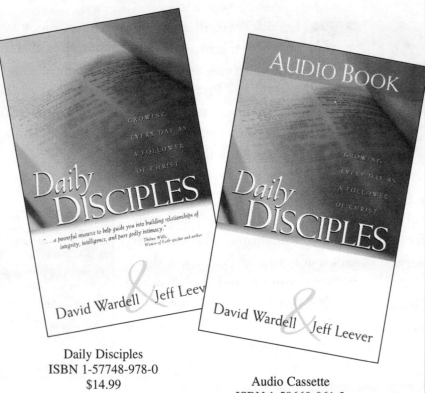

Daily Disciples
ISBN 1-57748-978-0
$14.99

Audio Cassette
ISBN 1-58660-061-3
$14.99

# AVAILABLE
# WHEREVER BOOKS ARE SOLD